Toxic Habits Kill Opportunities

By

Brenda Diann Johnson

ASWIFTT ENTERPRISES, LLC
Duncanville, Texas 75138

Copyright © 2025 Brenda Diann Johnson

All rights reserved

No part of this book may be reproduced, stored in a retrieval system, or transmitted by any means, electronic, mechanical, photocopying, recording or otherwise, without written permission from the author.

Brenda Diann Johnson
E-mail: brendadiannjohnson@yahoo.com

Published by
ASWIFTT ENTERPRISES, LLC
Imprint: ASWIFTT BOOKS
P.O. Box 380669
Duncanville, Texas 75138-0669

ISBN: 979-8-9901107-9-3

Library of Congress Control Number: 2025941900

Printed in the United States of America

Scripture references are taken from the King James Version of the Bible. In some instances, other versions of the Bible are used.

Cover Design and Editing by Brenda Diann Johnson

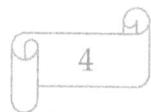

Dedications

Toxic Habits Kill Opportunities is dedicated to those who want to be fully transformed by the renewing of their minds and who want to fulfill their God-Ordained Purpose.

Acknowledgments

I acknowledge an Almighty God who gave me the passion, creativity, ideas, and inventions to educate the masses. I am determined to be a good steward.

Table of Contents

Dedications..................................5
Acknowledgments........................6
Introduction..............................11

Chapter I Ungrateful.......................15
Chapter II Abuse Access....................23
Chapter III Cheater........................31
Chapter IV Cause Drama.....................37
Chapter V Gossiper.........................45

Chapter VI Hypocrite.......................53
Chapter VII Liar...........................61
Chapter VIII Thief.........................69
Chapter IX Lazy............................77
Chapter X Coveter..........................83

Chapter XI Busybody........................89
Chapter XII Conspirer......................97
Chapter XIII Reject Knowledge.......105
Chapter XIV Selfishness................111
Chapter XV Jealous & Envious........117

Chapter XVI Greedy........................125
Chapter XVII Wicked.......................133
Chapter XVIII Manipulator.................141
Chapter XIX Promiscuous...................147
Chapter XX Angry..........................155

Conclusion	163
About the Author	169
Books and Services	171

Introduction

Introduction

It is widely acknowledged that our choices, whether positive or negative, play a significant role in determining the outcomes we encounter throughout our lives. As defined by dictionary.com, a habit refers to a behavioral pattern acquired through repetition until it becomes nearly automatic. Toxic habits are harmful behaviors or patterns that adversely impact an individual's life, relationships, and spiritual health. These detrimental habits often arise from factors such as selfishness, pride, dissatisfaction, or insufficient self-discipline and can hinder personal development and spiritual growth. It is essential for us to strive towards becoming the best versions of ourselves. By concentrating on enhancing our inner selves, we initiate the necessary transformation to cultivate harmonious relationships. The elimination of toxic habits not only prevents us from inadvertently hurting those around us but also protects our chances for progress in both personal and professional spheres.

Toxic habits have the potential to undermine prospects, isolate connections, and convert promising opportunities into unproductive routes. To progress effectively, we must recognize that our actions can either create possibilities or close them off. It is imperative that we understand how to conduct ourselves suitably in various personal and professional contexts. This book will delve into twenty (20) toxic behaviors that deprive us of valuable opportunities. Each chapter will outline and explain each habit, discuss the reasons these behaviors are detrimental, and emphasize the necessity of addressing them. Additionally, biblical examples illustrating the repercussions of such behaviors will be provided. We will also explore practical steps aimed at eradicating these habits and transitioning towards a healthier and more rewarding existence.

Let us begin this journey of self-discovery, change, and personal development. Through thoughtful reflection and actionable steps, we can shed what hinders our progress and welcome a path filled with opportunity and harmony.

Ungrateful

Chapter I
Ungrateful

To lack gratitude signifies an absence of appreciation for the kindness, assistance, or blessings one has received. An ungrateful individual tends to ignore the positives in their life, concentrating instead on what is missing. This behavior can manifest as complaints, a sense of entitlement, or a failure to recognize the sacrifices made by others. Often, ungratefulness stems from pride and selfishness, blinding a person to the worth of what they already have.

Exhibiting ungrateful behavior is inappropriate as it disrespects both God and fellow humans. When an individual chooses not to express gratitude, it undermines the efforts of those who have provided support or blessings. A lack of thankfulness also cultivates negativity that spreads dissatisfaction and resentment. Such attitudes can damage relationships since people may feel undervalued or overlooked. Most importantly, it dismisses God's gifts and provisions, which constitutes a form of disobedience toward Him.

Addressing the tendency towards ungratefulness is essential for achieving a joyful and content existence. Practicing gratitude enables individuals to recognize the daily blessings in their lives and fosters humility by acknowledging that all good things originate from God. By overcoming ungratefulness, people can forge stronger relationships, attain greater peace, and cultivate a more optimistic perspective on life. A grateful disposition enhances faith and inspires generosity toward others. Failing to address this issue allows ungratefulness to evolve into selfishness, envy, and unhappiness.

    A biblical illustration of ungratefulness is found in Luke 17:11–19 with the account of ten lepers. Jesus healed all ten men afflicted with leprosy; however, only one returned to express gratitude. The other nine received healing but did not acknowledge the miracle with thanks. This story highlights how prevalent ungratefulness can be and how it displeases God. Jesus praised the solitary individual who showed appreciation, underscoring the significance of gratitude and humility.

    The practice of ungratefulness can be countered through daily expressions of thankfulness and contentment. Individuals may begin by maintaining a journal detailing their blessings, showing appreciation towards others, and engaging in prayer filled with gratitude. Shifting focus from what one lacks to recognizing existing joys fosters a spirit of thankfulness. Surrounding oneself with positive influences and serving others also nurtures appreciation. By integrating gratitude into daily life practices, individuals can combat ungratefulness while embracing joy, humility, and tranquility.

Ungratefulness

Definition:
Ungratefulness is the failure to acknowledge or value God's blessings, often leading to a sense of entitlement.

Why It Is Wrong:
Being ungrateful breeds discontent and dishonors God. As stated in 1 Thessalonians 5:18, "Give thanks in all circumstances; for this is God's will for you in Christ Jesus."

Why It Needs Correction:
A lack of gratitude can obscure our awareness of God's provisions and hinder our spiritual development.

Biblical Example:
The Israelites expressed dissatisfaction and complaints despite receiving God's care during their time in the wilderness (Numbers 14:2-4).

Eliminating the Habit:
1. Cultivate a habit of daily gratitude towards God for His blessings.
2. Concentrate on what you possess instead of what you are missing.
3. Show appreciation to others.

Reflection Questions:
1. Do I tend to dwell on my shortcomings rather than valuing what I have?
2. In what ways could practicing gratitude alter my viewpoint and emotional state?
3. What blessings am I neglecting to recognize lately?

Practical Exercises:
1. Maintain a daily gratitude journal where you list three things for which you are thankful.
2. Each morning, verbally thank God for specific blessings in your life.
3. Communicate your appreciation to someone who has had a positive influence on you.

Closing Prayer:
Lord, assist me in developing a grateful heart that acknowledges and expresses thanks for all Your blessings.

20

Abuse Access

Chapter II
Abuse Access

Abusing access refers to the improper use of authority, privilege, or opportunities entrusted to an individual. It takes place when a person exploits their position, resources, or relationships for personal gain or dishonest intentions. Rather than upholding the trust placed in them, someone who abuses access utilizes it in ways that may harm others or disproportionately benefit themselves. This behavior reflects a deficiency in integrity and accountability and can lead to the deterioration of relationships, communities, and even entire nations.

Such conduct is deemed unethical as it undermines trust and fosters injustice. When individuals misuse their access, they create imbalances that advantage themselves while disadvantaging others, resulting in harm, resentment, and fractured connections. Abusing access also indicates a disregard for authority and for divine principles that encourage honesty and fairness. Ultimately, this behavior cultivates corruption and dishonor instead of promoting truthfulness and righteousness.

Addressing the tendency to abuse access is crucial for fostering trust, integrity, and fairness. When individuals handle their access with responsibility, they enhance relationships and exemplify good character. Ensuring accountability is vital since unchecked abuse can lead to increased dishonesty and corruption. By rectifying this behavior, individuals cultivate responsibility, stewardship, and respect for the opportunities afforded to them. A heart aligned with correction values fairness and leverages privilege for positive outcomes rather than negative ones.

A biblical illustration of abusing access is found in the story of Eli's sons, Hophni and Phinehas. In 1 Samuel 2:12–17, these priests exploited their sacred role by claiming the choicest portions of sacrifices meant for God while showing disrespect towards the people's offerings. Their actions stemmed from greed and disdain for divine commandments. As a consequence of their misuse of privilege, God imposed severe judgment upon them; both sons ultimately perished in battle. This narrative illustrates how misusing positions of privilege can lead to dire consequences.

To eliminate the habit of abusing access requires practicing humility, accountability, and respect toward others. Individuals must acknowledge that all privileges come from God and should be utilized for service rather than exploitation. Seeking wise counsel, ensuring transparency in decision-making processes, and nurturing an attitude of gratitude are essential steps in preventing abuse. By committing to honesty and stewardship practices, individuals can harness their access to uplift others while honoring God—thereby replacing corruption with integrity and self-interest with service.

Abusing Access

Definition
Abusing access refers to the inappropriate use of authority, privileges, or opportunities for personal advantage or to cause harm.

Why It Is Wrong
Misuse of access negatively impacts others, undermines trust, and disrespects God's provisions. According to Luke 12:48, "From everyone who has been given much, much will be demanded; and from the one who has been entrusted with much, much more will be asked."

Why It Needs Correction
If this behavior is not addressed, it can result in corruption, a decline in credibility, and eventual judgment.

Biblical Example
An illustration of this is seen with Potiphar's wife, who attempted to coerce Joseph for her own desires; however, Joseph chose not to exploit his access (Genesis 39:6-20).

Eliminating the Habit
1. Acknowledge and respect established boundaries and privileges.
2. Utilize positions of trust for service rather than exploitation.

    3. Seek accountability and guidance when facing temptation.

Reflection Questions
1. Have I ever misused trust or authority for my own benefit?
2. How can I honor God through my access and opportunities?
3. Who might benefit from the access that God has provided me?

Practical Exercises
1. Identify the privileges or opportunities that God has entrusted to you.
2. Make a commitment to use one of these opportunities for service this week.
3. Pray for wisdom to maintain integrity in all your responsibilities.

Closing Prayer
Lord, please assist me in honoring the trust and access You provide by using it to positively impact others and bring glory to You.

Cheater

Chapter III
Cheater

A cheater is someone who seeks to gain an unfair advantage through dishonest means. This can manifest in various forms, such as deceit, theft, plagiarism, or failing to acknowledge the contributions of others. Cheating extends beyond academic settings or games; it can infiltrate everyday life, personal relationships, and professional environments. When an individual claims credit for another's work or manipulates circumstances for their benefit, they engage in the harmful practice of cheating.

The act of cheating is fundamentally wrong as it undermines trust and integrity. It demonstrates a lack of respect not only for those who are unjustly treated but also for the cheaters themselves. This behavior often leaves others feeling misled or undervalued. Over time, dishonesty can tarnish reputations and damage interpersonal relationships. Even if unnoticed by others, cheating contravenes moral and ethical principles, ultimately resulting in adverse outcomes.

To cultivate character, honesty, and fairness, it is essential to rectify the habit of cheating. Individuals cannot truly progress or achieve success if their accomplishments stem from dishonesty. Genuine learning and personal development arise from dedication, persistence, and integrity. By addressing this habit, individuals learn accountability for their actions, acknowledge others' contributions, and adopt a lifestyle that fosters mutual respect. Without intervention, cheating transforms into a pervasive cycle that affects all aspects of life.

A Biblical example illustrating cheating is found in the narrative of Jacob and Esau. In Genesis 27, Jacob deceived his father Isaac with assistance from his mother Rebekah to receive a blessing that rightfully belonged to Esau, the firstborn son. This deceitful act led to familial discord and enduring conflict between the brothers. The account illustrates how cheating may yield immediate success but ultimately inflict pain and fractures relationships.

Eliminating the tendency to cheat involves embracing honesty and accountability. Individuals must learn to appreciate hard work, acknowledge their errors openly, and value others' efforts. Cultivating integrity entails opting for truthfulness even when deception appears more convenient. Engaging in prayer, self-reflection, and surrounding oneself with trustworthy influences can further bolster one's character. Overcoming cheating demands consistent effort; however, leading a life rooted in truthfulness brings peace along with trust and respect from peers.

Cheating

Definition
Cheating refers to the act of being dishonest or misleading in order to obtain an unfair advantage in various aspects of life.

Why It Is Wrong
Cheating undermines trust, harms relationships, and disrespects God. According to Proverbs 11:1, "The Lord detests dishonest scales, but accurate weights are his delight." Additionally, Luke 16:10 cautions that "Whoever can be trusted with very little can also be trusted with much; and whoever is dishonest with very little will also be dishonest with much."

Why It Needs Correction
If not addressed, cheating can develop into a harmful habit that diminishes integrity and hinders spiritual development.

Biblical Example
Jacob's deception of his father Isaac to appropriate Esau's blessing led to prolonged conflict within the family (Genesis 27:1-40).

Eliminating the Habit:
1. Acknowledge instances of dishonesty before God.
2. Seek support from a reliable friend or mentor for accountability.

3. Make it a daily practice to be honest in both minor and significant decisions.

Reflection Questions:
1. In what areas of my life am I tempted to cheat?
2. How has dishonesty impacted my relationships or faith?
3. What actions can I take today to uphold integrity?

Practical Exercises:
1. Compose a prayer admitting any instances of dishonesty.
2. Pledge to perform one act of integrity this week.
3. Confide in a trusted believer about one struggle and request accountability.

Closing Prayer:
Lord, grant me the strength to live truthfully and maintain integrity, resisting all temptations to cheat. Help me honor You in every aspect of my life.

Cause Drama

Chapter IV
Cause Drama

Causing drama refers to the act of creating unnecessary disputes, instigating arguments, or fostering discord among individuals. A person who engages in dramatic behavior typically gossips, amplifies issues, or manipulates circumstances to attract attention. This tendency thrives on conflict and undermines harmony within relationships, families, and communities. Rather than encouraging understanding and unity, causing drama cultivates division and confusion.

This behavior is detrimental as it harms relationships and erodes trust. Drama consumes valuable time and energy that could be directed towards constructive activities. It frequently spreads misinformation, results in misunderstandings, and pits individuals against each other. Those who instigate drama often exhibit immaturity and a lack of self-control, preferring chaos over tranquility. Most importantly, it contradicts the divine mandate to live harmoniously and love one another.

Addressing the habit of causing drama is essential for fostering peace, trust, and mutual respect among individuals. When people learn to manage their words and actions effectively, they contribute to an environment characterized by cooperation and kindness. By modifying this behavior, individuals can prevent unnecessary conflicts while strengthening their interpersonal connections. Developing skills such as attentive listening, respectful communication, and mature conflict resolution fosters a positive and healthy atmosphere. Without intervention, drama persists, resulting in fractured friendships and increased division.

A biblical illustration of causing drama is found in Korah's rebellion described in Numbers 16. Korah and his followers challenged Moses' authority by asserting their claim for equal standing with him and Aaron. Their actions incited discord among the Israelites, leading many to question Moses' leadership capabilities. As a consequence of their rebellion, God judged Korah's group by causing the earth to open up beneath them. This narrative underscores the severe repercussions of inciting unnecessary conflict.

The tendency to create drama can be overcome through the practice of self-discipline, humility, and peacemaking efforts. Individuals must cultivate the habit of pausing before speaking, steering clear of gossiping behaviors while concentrating on resolving disputes rather than igniting them. Engaging in prayerful reflection on scripture can foster patience and kindness when interacting with others. Additionally, surrounding oneself with positive influences can diminish the urge to participate in dramatic situations. By prioritizing peace over conflict, individuals can eradicate drama from their lives while nurturing healthier relationships that align with spiritual principles.

Causing Drama

Definition: Causing drama refers to the act of generating conflict, tension, or unwarranted emotional distress within relationships.

Why It Is Problematic: Engaging in drama disrupts harmony, fractures communities, and goes against God's call for unity. Proverbs 6:16-19 highlights that "There are six things the Lord detests, seven that are abominable to Him... a person who incites conflict within the community."

Reasons for Correction: Drama damages relationships, creates stress, and obstructs spiritual development.

Biblical Example: Absalom instigated a rebellion against his father King David, leading to national chaos (2 Samuel 15:1-12).

Eliminating the Habit:
1. Exercise self-discipline and take a moment before reacting.
2. Steer clear of gossip and refrain from spreading rumors.
3. Encourage reconciliation and promote peace in your relationships.

Reflection Questions:
1. In what instances have I contributed to unnecessary conflicts?
2. How can I foster peace during tense moments?

3. What actions can I take to prevent creating drama?

Practical Exercises:
1. Reflect on a recent dramatic situation and consider how you might have responded differently.
2. Commit to maintaining neutrality or calmness during conflicts this week.
3. Pray for tranquility in relationships marked by tension.

Closing Prayer:
Lord, grant me a serene spirit and enable me to introduce peace rather than discord into all my relationships.

Gossiper

Chapter V
Gossiper

To gossip refers to the act of disseminating rumors or discussing someone else's private affairs without their consent or awareness. This behavior typically involves embellishments, partial truths, or inaccuracies that can tarnish reputations and instigate unwarranted conflict. Although a gossiper may seem to be merely relaying information, they are actually fostering discord and violating trust. Engaging in gossip is a harmful practice that negatively impacts both the individual spreading the rumors and the subject of those rumors.

Gossiping is ethically wrong as it undermines trust and community cohesion. It damages interpersonal relationships, propagates negativity, and inflicts emotional distress on those targeted. Once spoken, words cannot be retracted, and gossip often extends well beyond its initial context. Such behavior also signals a deficiency in self-discipline and compassion since it opts to diminish others rather than uplift them. Most critically, gossip contradicts divine principles; religious teachings encourage believers to communicate truthfully and supportively.

Addressing the tendency to gossip is vital for fostering peace, trust, and respect within relationships. When individuals refrain from gossiping, they uphold the dignity of others and cultivate an atmosphere conducive to honesty and kindness. Modifying this behavior also enhances self-control and instructs people on managing information judiciously. If left unchecked, gossip perpetuates division and distrust, resulting in fractured friendships and emotional scars. A person who actively works to eliminate this habit demonstrates maturity and integrity.

A biblical illustration of gossip can be found with Miriam and Aaron in Numbers 12:1–10, where they spoke ill of Moses due to his Cushite wife while questioning his leadership as God's appointed figure. Their remarks constituted gossip that fostered doubt and dishonor. Consequently, God reprimanded Miriam by afflicting her with leprosy for seven days. This narrative underscores how displeasing gossip is to God and highlights the severe repercussions of unjustly speaking against others.

The practice of gossip can be curtailed through the cultivation of self-control, kindness, and respect for others. Individuals should learn to reflect carefully before voicing their thoughts by considering whether their comments are constructive or detrimental. Opting to pray for others instead of discussing them negatively serves as another effective strategy against gossip. Additionally, surrounding oneself with positive influences while steering clear of discussions that promote gossip further aids in breaking this cycle. By choosing words rooted in truthfulness, encouragement, and love, individuals can supplant gossip with peace while honoring God through their communication.

Gossiping

Definition: Gossiping refers to discussing others in a detrimental or harmful manner, frequently involving the dissemination of rumors or confidential information.

Why It Is Wrong: Engaging in gossip can tarnish reputations, damage relationships, and undermine the church community. Proverbs 16:28 cautions that "A perverse person stirs up conflict, and a gossip separates close friends."

Why It Needs Correction: Gossip fosters division, diminishes trust, and obstructs spiritual growth.

Biblical Example: Miriam and Aaron criticized Moses, leading to divine retribution (Numbers 12:1-10).

Eliminating the Habit:
1. Focus on sharing uplifting and encouraging words instead of criticism.
2. Refrain from relaying negative remarks.
3. Exercise discernment regarding what information is shared.

Reflection Questions:
1. In what instances have I participated in gossip?
2. How has gossip negatively impacted my relationships or spiritual journey?
3. What steps can I take to transform my speech to uplift others?

Practical Exercises:
1. Pay attention to your discussions for any negative commentary about others.
2. Substitute one instance of gossip with an encouraging remark today.
3. Pray for those whom you might be inclined to speak ill of.

Closing Prayer:
Lord, please protect my speech and guide me to use words that uplift and encourage rather than tear down.

Hypocrite

Chapter VI
Hypocrite

A hypocrite is someone who claims to uphold moral principles, values, or beliefs that they do not genuinely embody. Hypocrisy involves the tendency to articulate one thing while acting in contradiction, often to project an image of righteousness or seek validation from others. A hypocrite may criticize others for faults they themselves possess or maintain a deceptive facade to conceal their true actions. This behavior stems from dishonesty and arrogance, undermining both personal integrity and trust with others.

Hypocritical behavior is problematic as it misleads people and distorts reality. When individuals behave hypocritically, they create an impression of superiority while secretly engaging in similar or more egregious actions. This leads to confusion, resentment, and a breakdown of trust in interpersonal relationships. Furthermore, hypocrisy disrespects God, who perceives the truth within one's heart rather than mere external appearances. A hypocrite exists in a falsehood that contradicts God's call for honesty and authenticity.

Addressing the tendency toward hypocrisy is crucial since truthfulness and genuineness are vital for fostering healthy relationships and promoting spiritual development. Individuals should learn to acknowledge their challenges and strive for improvement instead of concealing them behind a façade. By overcoming hypocrisy, people can become more reliable, humble, and sincere. This transformation enables them to support others through transparency rather than feigning perfection. Moreover, rectifying hypocrisy aligns with God's desire for truthfulness at the core of one's being.

An illustrative example of hypocrisy appears in the Bible with the Pharisees. In Matthew 23, Jesus admonished them for their duplicitous conduct. While they outwardly adhered to religious customs, their inner selves were rife with pride, avarice, and corruption. Jesus likened them to "whitewashed tombs," attractive externally yet filled with decay internally. This serves as a demonstration that God denounces hypocrisy and prioritizes heartfelt sincerity over superficial appearances.

The pattern of hypocrisy can be eradicated by embracing honesty, humility, and introspection. Individuals need to live in alignment with the values they profess to hold dear by acknowledging their vulnerabilities rather than concealing them. Engaging in prayer, seeking repentance, and fostering accountability can bolster integrity while diminishing the inclination to deceive. By embracing authenticity, people can cultivate trustworthiness, strengthen relationships, and honor God effectively. A life lived without hypocrisy fosters freedom, tranquility, and spiritual advancement.

Hypocrisy

Definition:
Hypocrisy involves professing to follow God or lead a righteous life while secretly engaging in actions that contradict His principles.

Why It Is Wrong:
Hypocrisy misleads others, undermines one's credibility, and displeases God. According to Matthew 23:27-28, "Woe to you, teachers of the law and Pharisees, you hypocrites! You are like whitewashed tombs, which appear beautiful on the outside but are filled with the bones of the dead and all things unclean on the inside."

Why It Needs Correction:
This behavior hinders authentic spiritual growth and negatively impacts one's testimony.

Biblical Example:
The Pharisees showcased an outward appearance of righteousness while being corrupt internally (Matthew 23:1-36).

Eliminating the Habit:
1. Acknowledge inconsistencies and seek repentance.
2. Strive to live genuinely in accordance with God's Word.
3. Pursue accountability for aligning both private and public lives.

Reflection Questions:
1. In what ways might I be displaying hypocrisy?
2. How can I ensure my private behaviors reflect my public faith?
3. Who can support me in maintaining an authentic lifestyle?

Practical Exercises:
1. Identify one specific area where your actions do not align with your claimed beliefs.
2. Take a concrete step to rectify this within the week.
3. Pray daily for integrity in thoughts, words, and actions.

Closing Prayer:
Lord, assist me in living authentically before You and others, allowing Your truth to shine through every aspect of my life.

Liar

Chapter VII
Liar

A liar is defined as an individual who deliberately conveys false information, misleads others, or obscures the truth. Lying can take various forms, such as exaggerating facts, concealing misconduct, or providing false testimony against someone else. At its core, lying represents a conscious choice to abandon honesty for self-preservation or personal gain. Though a lie may seem minor or harmless at first glance, the habit of lying creates a cycle of deceit that ultimately damages both one's character and interpersonal relationships.

Deception is viewed as unethical because it diminishes trust and fosters confusion. When people engage in dishonest behavior, they mislead others and create false perceptions that can lead to real harm. Particularly concerning is false testimony, which can wrongfully accuse or condemn innocent individuals. Lies erode healthy relationships and cause divisions within families, communities, and workplaces. Most importantly, dishonesty stands in direct opposition to the divine call for truthfulness and righteousness.

Confronting the tendency to lie is vital since honesty is fundamental to integrity. Without truthfulness, trust, peace, and justice cannot thrive. When individuals commit themselves to truthful communication, they show respect for others and accept their responsibilities. Correcting dishonest behavior not only strengthens one's character but also helps prevent future transgressions because lies are often used to cover up wrongdoing. Living authentically leads to freedom; conversely, a life rooted in deceit breeds bondage and guilt.

An example of deception is illustrated in the New Testament through the story of Ananias and Sapphira found in Acts 5:1–11. This couple sold property but secretly kept part of the money while pretending to donate the entire amount to the apostles. Their duplicity was aimed not just at church leaders but also at God Himself. As a result of their dishonesty, both faced immediate death as divine punishment—highlighting the seriousness of lying and giving false testimony before God.

The inclination to lie can be overcome by fostering honesty, practicing confession, and taking responsibility for one's actions. It is important for individuals to prioritize truth over personal advantage and understand that lies ultimately cause more significant harm. Establishing a daily commitment to speak truthfully—even about small matters—reinforces integrity. Engaging in prayer, repentance, and studying Scripture can aid in transforming one's heart and mind toward honesty. By adopting a lifestyle centered around truthfulness, individuals honor God, earn respect from others, and build a reputation for dependability.

Lying

Definition:
Lying refers to the deliberate act of conveying false information or misleading others, which encompasses being a false witness.

Why It Is Wrong:
Lying undermines trust, harms relationships, and is displeasing to God. Proverbs 12:22 states, "The Lord detests lying lips, but he delights in people who are trustworthy."

Why It Needs Correction:
Regularly engaging in deceit erodes credibility, induces guilt, and hinders spiritual development.

Biblical Example:
Ananias and Sapphira deceived regarding their contribution and suffered severe consequences for their dishonesty (Acts 5:1-11).

Eliminating the Habit:
1. Acknowledge your lies to God and ask for His forgiveness.
2. Dedicate yourself to honesty in every aspect of life, even under challenging circumstances.
3. Establish accountability with a reliable friend.

Reflection Questions:
1. In what situations have I lied to escape repercussions?

2. How has dishonesty impacted my relationships or faith?
3. What truths should I express today?

Practical Exercises:
1. Keep a journal of instances where you felt tempted to deceive and pray for fortitude.
2. Choose one situation where you typically avoid honesty and commit to speaking the truth.
3. Request that a dependable friend help hold you accountable for your honesty.

Closing Prayer:
Heavenly Father, guide me to speak with truthfulness and uphold integrity, reflecting Your character in all my words.

Thief

Chapter VIII
Thief

A thief is defined as an individual who unlawfully takes possessions that do not belong to them, without consent or legal right. Theft can encompass a range of items including money, physical property, intellectual property, and even time. The propensity to steal stems from selfishness and greed, reflecting a lack of respect for the rights and efforts of others. Acts of theft can vary in scale; they may be minor infractions like taking something without asking or significant crimes such as robbing someone of valuable belongings. In any case, stealing is a harmful behavior that adversely affects both the perpetrator and the victim.

The act of thievery is fundamentally wrong because it breaches trust, inflicts harm, and contravenes God's commandment: "You shall not steal" (Exodus 20:15). Theft fosters an environment of fear, insecurity, and discord within families, workplaces, and communities. It often leads to resentment among victims who have been treated unjustly. Additionally, engaging in theft undermines one's character by substituting honesty with deceitfulness. Ultimately, stealing alienates individuals from God as it embodies dishonesty, covetousness, and defiance against His will.

It is crucial to address the tendency to steal because integrity is built on honesty and fosters peace. Individuals must cultivate respect for others' property rights to establish trust. Without intervention, a thief may escalate their behavior as greed and dishonesty intensify. Addressing the issue of theft promotes responsibility and accountability while offering a chance to mend what has been damaged. Living honestly enables individuals to forge stronger connections while freeing themselves from feelings of guilt or shame.

An illustrative example of theft in biblical context is found in the story of Achan. In Joshua 7, following the conquest of Jericho, God instructed the Israelites not to take any devoted items for themselves. Nevertheless, Achan covertly took a beautiful robe along with silver and gold and concealed them in his tent. His actions led not only to personal judgment but also adversely affected the entire nation by causing Israel's defeat in their subsequent battle. This narrative demonstrates that stealing carries significant repercussions for both the thief and those impacted by their actions.

The inclination toward thievery can be overcome through fostering contentment, honesty, and accountability. Individuals should learn to rely on God for their needs rather than appropriating what belongs to others. Engaging in repentance, confession, and making amends where feasible can disrupt the cycle of theft. Cultivating self-control and gratitude further fortifies one's resolve against greed. By embracing honesty and respecting others' rights, individuals can transform their lives from one marked by theft into one characterized by integrity that honors both God and fellow humans.

Stealing

Definition:
Stealing refers to the act of taking something that does not belong to you, which can include physical items, intellectual property, or even someone's time.

Why It Is Wrong:
The act of stealing goes against divine commandments and causes harm to others. As stated in Exodus 20:15, "You shall not steal."

Why It Needs Correction:
Engaging in theft undermines trust, creates feelings of guilt, and negatively impacts both spiritual and interpersonal relationships.

Biblical Example:
Achan violated God's command by taking forbidden items from Jericho, leading to Israel's defeat (Joshua 7:1-26).

Eliminating the Habit:
1. Acknowledge the wrongdoing by confessing and returning stolen items or providing restitution.
2. Cultivate a sense of contentment with what God has given you.
3. Commit to honesty and integrity in every aspect of life.

Reflection Questions:
1. Have I taken things that aren't mine, even in minor instances?

2. In what ways has stealing impacted my conscience or my relationships?
3. How can I foster practices of honesty and contentment?

Practical Exercises:
1. Return or offer restitution for something wrongfully taken.
2. Contemplate God's provision and express thankfulness.
3. Engage in daily prayer for integrity in all interactions.

Closing Prayer:
Lord, guide me to respect others and You by living a life rooted in honesty and integrity across all aspects of my existence.

Lazy

Chapter IX
Lazy

Laziness refers to the reluctance to exert effort when it is necessary. An individual exhibiting laziness tends to evade responsibilities, postpone critical tasks, and often opts for comfort over discipline. This behavior manifests as procrastination, idleness, and a lack of self-regulation. Consequently, it hinders individuals from achieving their objectives and prevents them from utilizing their time and skills effectively.

Engaging in lazy behavior is detrimental as it results in squandered opportunities and unrealized potential. When a person chooses to be lazy, they overlook their obligations, allowing significant work to accumulate. This accumulation can lead to stress, setbacks, and disappointment. Additionally, laziness impacts others by compelling them to take on the responsibilities that the lazy individual neglects. Ultimately, a consistent pattern of laziness can result in poverty, stagnation, and eroded trust.

Addressing the issue of laziness is crucial since success and advancement are attainable only through discipline and dedicated effort. Individuals cannot fulfill their aspirations if they resist taking action. It is imperative to substitute laziness with constructive habits like establishing goals, adhering to schedules, and being accountable for one's duties. By doing so, individuals cultivate self-esteem, build character, and demonstrate responsibility towards others. A life characterized by discipline fosters productivity and fulfillment.

The Bible illustrates the concept of laziness in Proverbs 24:30–34, which depicts a slothful man's field overrun with thorns and crumbling walls. His negligence resulted in the deterioration of his land leading to ruin. This narrative highlights the damaging effects of idleness and emphasizes how failure to engage in work leads to poverty and adversity. The scripture cautions against laziness as it poses significant harm that should be avoided.

To overcome the tendency toward laziness, one must cultivate self-discipline by establishing daily routines and resisting procrastination. Taking small steps such as completing assignments promptly, minimizing distractions, and maintaining motivation through prayer or encouragement can facilitate this process. Moreover, surrounding oneself with industrious individuals can foster better habits. By replacing lethargy with diligence, people can honor God while fulfilling their commitments and attaining enduring success in life.

Laziness

Definition: Laziness refers to the tendency to evade work, effort, or accountability, often characterized by procrastination and a lack of self-discipline.

Why It Is Problematic: Laziness obstructs personal advancement, spiritual growth, and the fulfillment of God's intentions for our lives. As stated in Proverbs 13:4, "The soul of the sluggard craves and gets nothing, while the soul of the diligent is richly supplied."

Need for Correction: Laziness results in lost opportunities, unrealized potential, and a standstill in spiritual development.

Biblical Example: Proverbs 6:6-11 advises us to "Go to the ant, you sluggard; consider its ways and be wise!" This highlights that diligence fosters abundance and blessings.

Strategies for Overcoming Laziness:
1. Establish daily objectives and timelines.
2. Initiate tasks promptly instead of postponing them.
3. Cultivate consistent discipline through managing minor responsibilities.

Reflection Questions:
1. In what aspects of my life does laziness have an impact?
2. What emotions do I experience as a result of procrastination?

3. What actionable steps can I implement to enhance my diligence?

Practical Exercises:
1. Organize your day with specific, achievable tasks.
2. Immediately tackle one task you have been putting off.
3. Maintain a nightly journal to monitor progress and contemplate improvements.

Closing Prayer:
Lord, grant me the vigor and discipline necessary to act diligently and honor You through my efforts and time.

/ **Coveter**

Chapter X
Coveter

To covet signifies possessing an intense and unhealthy longing for something that belongs to someone else. This feeling transcends mere desire; it manifests as a powerful yearning that frequently gives rise to jealousy, resentment, and immoral actions. Such a mindset can lead individuals to overlook their own blessings and may result in harmful behaviors like theft, deceit, or even homicide. While coveting originates in the heart, it ultimately reveals itself through detrimental actions.

The act of coveting is considered wrong because it invites sin and chaos into one's life. A person who persistently yearns for what others possess often finds themselves discontented and unhappy. This behavior can harm relationships by fostering envy, animosity, and strife. In severe instances, it may compel individuals to engage in criminal acts such as stealing or killing to fulfill their desires. The Bible cautions against coveting as it taints the heart and distances individuals from divine intentions.

Overcoming the tendency to covet is essential for achieving a life characterized by peace, gratitude, and virtue. When individuals cease their covetous thoughts, they begin to value their own fortunes and cultivate contentment. Letting go of these desires enables them to form healthy, loving connections devoid of jealousy or envy. A heart liberated from coveting can concentrate on generosity, kindness, and loyalty. Without intervention, however, this habit can escalate into more significant transgressions and wreak havoc on many lives.

An illustrative example of coveting is found in the story of King David in the Bible. In 2 Samuel 11, David's desire for Bathsheba—Uriah's wife—led him down a path of adultery and ultimately prompted him to orchestrate Uriah's death during combat. This episode illustrates how unchecked desire can escalate into fatal actions with far-reaching repercussions for both personal relationships and his kingdom.

To eradicate the habit of coveting, one should practice gratitude, self-discipline, and trust in God's provisions. It is vital for individuals to recognize their own possessions rather than measuring themselves against others. Engaging in prayer, studying scripture, and contemplating divine commandments can fortify one's heart against feelings of envy. Choosing generosity while rejoicing in others' successes also aids in replacing covetousness with love. By adopting an attitude of thankfulness combined with self-control, people can conquer this detrimental habit of coveting and achieve genuine contentment.

Coveting

Definition: Coveting refers to a strong yearning for what others possess, which can often result in feelings of jealousy or lead to harmful actions.

Why It Is Wrong: Engaging in coveting breeds feelings of dissatisfaction and greed, constituting a sin that contravenes God's commandment as stated in Exodus 20:17: "You shall not covet your neighbor's house; you shall not desire your neighbor's wife, or his male or female servant, his ox or donkey, or anything that belongs to your neighbor."

Why It Needs Correction: The act of coveting can cultivate bitterness and resentment, potentially escalating into destructive behaviors.

Biblical Example: An instance of coveting can be seen with King Ahab, who desired Naboth's vineyard and plotted its acquisition, which ultimately led to sin and divine judgment (1 Kings 21:1-16).

Eliminating the Habit:
1. Cultivate contentment with what God has given (Philippians 4:11-13).
2. Rejoice in the successes and blessings of others.
3. Steer clear of comparisons and concentrate on gratitude.

Reflection Questions:
1. In which aspects do I find myself struggling with coveting?
2. How does my envy influence my relationships and spiritual journey?
3. What blessings in my life can I choose to focus on instead?

Practical Exercises:
1. Daily note three things for which you are grateful.
2. Pray for someone toward whom you feel envy.
3. Take time each week to contemplate God's provisions in your life.

Closing Prayer:
Lord, assist me in finding satisfaction in Your gifts and guide me away from envy and covetousness.

Busybody

Chapter XI
Busybody

A busybody refers to someone who intrudes into the concerns of others, often engaging in issues that do not pertain to them. This tendency frequently entails gossiping, disseminating rumors, or intervening in situations without invitation. A busybody expends energy on other people's affairs instead of attending to their own obligations. Although they may think they are being helpful, their involvement typically results in more harm than benefit.

The act of meddling is detrimental as it generates confusion, fosters division, and harms relationships. Those who pry into others' lives often disclose information that isn't theirs to share, potentially leading to hurt feelings and eroded trust. Additionally, busybodies neglect their personal responsibilities while preoccupying themselves with matters that do not concern them. This behavior contradicts divine guidance for individuals to lead quiet lives, work diligently, and manage their own affairs.

Addressing the tendency to be a busybody is essential for fostering peace, respect, and accountability. When individuals concentrate on their personal development and obligations, they contribute to healthier dynamics within families and communities. Rectifying this behavior also aids in sidestepping unnecessary conflict and drama. Rather than interfering in others' lives, people can channel their time and energy toward constructive endeavors that enhance character and relationships.

The Bible provides an example of busybodies in 2 Thessalonians 3:11, where Paul cautions the church about certain individuals who were idle and disruptive—failing to work while instead becoming preoccupied with others' affairs. Rather than living quietly and striving for self-sufficiency, these individuals wasted time meddling in the lives of others. Paul urged believers to shun this conduct and exemplify disciplined and responsible living. This underscores the notion that Scripture regards being a busybody as counterproductive and harmful.

Overcoming the habit of being a busybody can be achieved through self-discipline, prioritizing one's own responsibilities, and concentrating on positive aspirations. Individuals must learn to resist the urge to interfere in matters outside their purview. Prayerful intent, discipline, and cultivating a robust work ethic can help shift focus away from gossiping and meddling towards personal growth and service. By upholding values such as respect, responsibility, and peace, individuals can break free from the busybody mentality while honoring God and benefiting others.

Busybody

Definition
A busybody refers to an individual who meddles in the lives of others, often providing unsolicited advice or involvement.

Reasons for Concern
Participating in busybody behavior can lead to conflicts, violate personal boundaries, and damage relationships. The scripture from 1 Thessalonians 4:11 advises us: "Make it your ambition to lead a quiet life: You should mind your own business and work with your hands, just as we instructed you."

Need for Change
Persistent interference obstructs the cultivation of healthy relationships and hampers individual growth.

Biblical Reference
The Corinthians were cautioned against engaging in matters that did not concern them (1 Corinthians 4:12-14).

Breaking the Habit:
1. Focus on your own duties.
2. Respect the privacy and boundaries of others.
3. Avoid giving unnecessary opinions on other people's issues.

Reflection Prompts:
1. In which situations have I intruded into matters that were not mine?
2. How can I shift my focus towards improving my own life instead of concerning myself with others?
3. What specific boundaries must I commit to respecting moving forward?

Practical Activities:
1. Recognize one area where you tend to intrude unnecessarily and make a conscious effort to withdraw.
2. Redirect your attention towards personal growth or community involvement.
3. Seek divine guidance in honoring others' boundaries through prayer.

Closing Prayer:
Lord, guide me in managing my own affairs while serving others with kindness, avoiding any form of unwarranted interference.

Conspirer

Chapter XII
Conspirer

To conspire refers to the act of secretly coordinating with others to inflict harm, deceive, or fulfill a self-serving agenda. A conspirer is an individual who operates covertly against another person, group, or even contrary to divine intentions. This behavior typically involves elements of deceit, betrayal, and dishonesty, rendering it harmful to both individuals and communities. Although such actions may initially appear concealed, the consequences of conspiring ultimately result in division, injury, and judgment.

Engaging in conspiracy is immoral as it stems from malicious intent and deceitfulness. It contradicts God's directive to love one another and live with integrity. Conspiring inflicts damage on innocent individuals and fosters distrust among family members, friends, or community associates. It represents a rebellious attitude that aims to accomplish objectives through falsehoods and clandestine schemes rather than through truthfulness and righteousness. Consequently, Scripture strongly denounces this conduct.

Addressing the tendency to conspire is essential for maintaining personal integrity, fostering peace, and promoting unity. Covert schemes and hidden motives bring ruin not only to those targeted but also to the conspirators themselves. If unaddressed, such behavior can lead to fractured relationships, feelings of guilt, and ultimately divine judgment. A life characterized by truthfulness, transparency, and righteousness negates the necessity for secrecy and harmful plotting. Corrective measures pave the way for peace, trustworthiness, and respect among individuals.

An illustration of conspiracy can be found in Genesis 37:18–20 in the Bible when Joseph's brothers plotted against him. Motivated by jealousy, they schemed to kill him before opting instead to sell him into slavery. Their hidden machinations resulted in years of suffering for Joseph; however, God eventually transformed this situation into something positive. This narrative underscores the gravity of conspiracy and its destructive potential when individuals act out of jealousy and hatred rather than love.

The tendency toward conspiring can be eradicated by cultivating honesty, humility, and love. Instead of engaging in secretive scheming, individuals should prioritize open communication, pursue peace actively, and resolve conflicts with integrity. Prayerful adherence to God's teachings enables believers to resist the temptation of devising evil plans against others. By upholding truthfulness, practicing forgiveness, and demonstrating love toward one another, people can break free from the damaging cycle of conspiracy while honoring God and fostering harmonious relationships.

Conspiring

Definition:
Conspiring refers to the covert planning or scheming with others to engage in wrongful actions or manipulate circumstances.

Why It Is Wrong:
Conspiracy leads to deception, betrayal, and harm inflicted on others. As stated in Psalm 64:6, "They plot injustice and utter harmful words; they deceive with their speech."

Why It Needs Correction:
If left unchecked, conspiracies can undermine trust, damage relationships, and jeopardize one's spiritual integrity.

Biblical Example:
Joseph's brothers plotted against him to sell him into slavery (Genesis 37:18-28).

Eliminating the Habit:
1. Confess any secret scheming to God.
2. Substitute deceit with openness and sincerity.
3. Pursue reconciliation where harm has occurred.

Reflection Questions:
1. Have I ever engaged in secretive plans that caused harm to others?
2. In what ways can I embody honesty in all my interactions?

3. Who do I need to reach out to for reconciliation?

Practical Exercises:
1. Reflect on any previous conspiracies and confess them to God.
2. Develop a strategy to rebuild trust with those impacted.
3. Pray for wisdom in acting with integrity.

Closing Prayer:
Lord, purify my heart from hidden plots and guide me toward acting with honesty and love.

Reject Knowledge

Chapter XIII
Reject Knowledge

Rejecting knowledge involves the refusal to engage in learning, the neglect of wisdom, and the dismissal of guidance. This behavior can manifest in various forms, including ignorance, impulsiveness, and defiance. A person who turns away from knowledge consciously opts to ignore truth and understanding, even when it is accessible. Rather than advancing in wisdom, they remain entrenched in detrimental habits that hinder their development.

The act of rejecting knowledge is detrimental as it results in poor decision-making and adverse outcomes. When individuals disregard wisdom, they often fail to perceive surrounding dangers and tend to repeat past errors. Such rejection also disrespects those who endeavor to educate and guide us. Furthermore, it can adversely impact others since ignorance and disobedience contribute to confusion and chaos. Without knowledge, people are susceptible to manipulation and unable to navigate life wisely.

To lead a fulfilling and successful life, it is crucial to overcome the tendency to reject knowledge. Embracing knowledge fosters growth, comprehension, and informed decision-making capabilities. Accepting knowledge enables individuals to cultivate discernment and maturity while equipping them with essential tools for overcoming obstacles and steering clear of harmful behaviors. By addressing this habit, individuals not only enhance their own lives but also positively influence their families, communities, and future generations.

A biblical illustration of rejecting knowledge is represented by King Saul. In 1 Samuel 15, God instructed Saul to annihilate the Amalekites along with all their possessions; however, Saul disobeyed by sparing the king's life and retaining the finest livestock. When confronted by the prophet Samuel about his actions, Saul attempted to justify his decisions instead of acknowledging his need for correction. His disregard for God's instruction ultimately led him to lose his kingdom—a narrative that underscores the grave repercussions of ignoring wisdom and guidance.

To eradicate the habit of rejecting knowledge, one must cultivate humility, obedience, and a readiness to learn. Individuals should take time before making decisions, seek wise counsel actively, and remain receptive to correction. Engaging with scripture through reading and reflection aids in developing wisdom and discernment. Additionally, surrounding oneself with mentors or positive influences fosters personal growth. By prioritizing knowledge rather than dismissing it outrightly, individuals can live more wisely, make improved choices, and achieve enduring success.

Rejecting Knowledge

Definition:
Rejecting knowledge refers to the tendency to overlook wisdom, education, or guidance, often driven by ignorance, impulsiveness, or defiance.

Why It Is Wrong:
Disregarding knowledge prevents us from making sound choices, can result in errors, and is displeasing to God. As stated in Proverbs 1:7, "The fear of the Lord is the beginning of knowledge; fools despise wisdom and instruction."

Why It Needs Correction:
Failing to correct this behavior can hinder personal, spiritual, and relational development.

Biblical Example:
King Saul disregarded God's commands and ignored Samuel's advice, which ultimately led to his demise (1 Samuel 15:10-23).

Eliminating the Habit:
1. Seek God's guidance humbly in every decision.

2. Engage with biblical wisdom through reading and application.

3. Be receptive to wise counsel from mentors and trustworthy believers.

Reflection Questions:
1. In what instances have I overlooked wise counsel that resulted in negative outcomes?
2. How can I purposefully pursue knowledge on a daily basis?
3. Which aspects of my life could benefit from further learning or correction?

Practical Exercises:
1. Read a chapter of Proverbs each day and contemplate its application in your life.
2. Request guidance from a mentor or pastor regarding a specific area of your life.
3. Keep a journal detailing lessons learned from moments when you dismissed wisdom.

Closing Prayer:
Lord, grant me the ability to value knowledge and wisdom, guiding me towards decisions that honor You.

/ **Selfishness**

Chapter XIV
Selfishness

To act selfishly entails prioritizing one's own needs, desires, and feelings over those of others, disregarding their well-being. A person who is selfish typically pursues personal gratification first, often at the cost of those around them. This behavior stems from self-absorption and a deficiency in empathy. When individuals exhibit selfishness, they tend to lack kindness, generosity, and love—qualities that are vital for nurturing healthy connections and adhering to divine principles.

Selfish behavior is considered wrong as it contradicts the divine directive to love others as we love ourselves. Such self-centeredness fosters division, greed, and neglect toward those who may require assistance. Rather than fostering unity, selfishness breeds discord and fractured relationships. The scriptures caution against living solely for personal benefit since this mindset obstructs the heart from engaging in service and compassion. A life centered on self leaves scant opportunity for God's love to be expressed through an individual towards others.

Addressing selfish tendencies is crucial because they undermine both individual integrity and communal trust. If unaddressed, selfishness can cultivate envy, greed, and even oppression of others. To achieve harmony and peace, individuals must learn to look beyond their own interests and consider the needs of those around them. Correction fosters a spirit marked by generosity, kindness, and humility—attributes that strengthen relationships and honor God.

An illustrative instance of selfishness in scripture appears in Luke 12:16–21 within the parable of the rich fool. In this narrative, a man with a plentiful harvest opts to construct larger barns for his surplus rather than sharing or utilizing it to assist others; he focuses solely on his comfort. God labels him a fool for hoarding treasures only for himself while neglecting spiritual richness. This tale highlights how selfishness can obscure one's understanding of generosity and spiritual duty.

The tendency towards selfishness can be countered by cultivating love, generosity, and gratitude. Instead of fixating on personal gain alone, individuals should actively seek out ways to serve others and give freely without anticipating reciprocation. Nurturing a grateful heart can help redirect focus from oneself to God and the needs of others. Through consistent prayer, humility, and everyday acts of kindness, selfish inclinations can be transformed into a spirit of giving that mirrors God's love and promotes peaceful relationships.

Selfishness

Definition:
Selfishness involves placing one's own desires above the needs and welfare of others.

Why It Is Wrong:
Engaging in selfish behavior damages relationships and disrespects God. As stated in Philippians 2:3, "Do nothing out of selfish ambition or vain conceit. Rather, in humility value others above yourselves."

Why It Needs Correction:
Self-serving tendencies lead to feelings of isolation, bitterness, and spiritual immaturity.

Biblical Example:
Ananias and Sapphira demonstrated selfishness with their offering (Acts 5:1-11).

Eliminating the Habit:
1. Cultivate generosity by serving those around you.
2. Reflect on daily decisions to identify any selfish intentions.
3. Pray for God to develop a selfless heart within you.

Reflection Questions:
1. In which areas do I display selfish behavior?
2. How can I focus on the needs of others this week?

3. In what ways does my selfishness obstruct my spiritual development?

Practical Exercises:
1. Carry out a kind deed without anticipating any reward.
2. Dedicate time, resources, or attention to someone who requires assistance.
3. Pray each day for a heart that prioritizes the welfare of others.

Closing Prayer:
Lord, help me learn to prioritize others over myself and to embody a spirit of selflessness.

Jealous & Envious

Chapter XV
Jealous & Envious

Jealousy and envy are harmful behaviors that can damage relationships and hinder personal development. Jealousy stems from the fear of losing something significant, such as love, attention, or status, to another person. In contrast, envy is characterized by the longing to possess what someone else has, like wealth, achievement, skills, or recognition. Although often mistakenly interchanged, jealousy is concerned with safeguarding what one already possesses, whereas envy emerges from a desire for what belongs to others. Both feelings originate from dissatisfaction and a lack of faith in God's provision.

The manifestations of jealousy and envy are detrimental because they breed bitterness, conflict, and division. These tendencies obstruct individuals from celebrating the achievements and blessings of others, substituting love with animosity. Such emotions can prompt harmful behaviors—slander, manipulation, or even violence—as evidenced throughout history and in religious texts. The Bible cautions against these attitudes since they stem from selfishness and pride instead of humility and love. They deprive individuals of peace and disrupt unity among people.

Addressing these behaviors is vital as they obstruct spiritual growth and harm interpersonal relationships. If not addressed, jealousy and envy can taint one's heart, resulting in persistent unhappiness and discontentment. Correcting these tendencies encourages gratitude, humility, and compassion. By learning to be satisfied with what God provides and trusting His timing, individuals can transform feelings of jealousy and envy into joy and tranquility. This transformation is crucial for fostering harmonious relationships with others while maintaining a faithful walk with God.

The Bible illustrates instances of jealousy and envy through various narratives. For example, in 1 Samuel 18:6–9, King Saul's jealousy towards David escalated after the people praised David's military successes more than his own; this growing jealousy ultimately evolved into hatred that drove Saul to attempt David's murder multiple times. Similarly, Genesis 37:11 depicts Joseph's brothers envying him due to his dreams and their father's favoritism toward him; their envy culminated in selling Joseph into slavery. These accounts highlight how jealousy and envy can lead to destructive decisions and fractured relationships.

To overcome jealousy and envy, one must cultivate gratitude, love, and trust in God. Rather than engaging in comparisons with others, it's essential to acknowledge personal blessings genuinely. Celebrating others' successes fosters unity and strengthens connections between individuals. Prayerfully seeking God's guidance can aid in transforming negative emotions into positive actions. By prioritizing love, humility, and contentment over negative feelings like jealousy or envy, individuals can foster a spirit of peace and generosity that contributes to a healthier and more fulfilling life.

Jealousy and Envy

Definition:
Jealousy refers to the resentment directed towards another person's advantages or relationships, whereas envy involves longing for what others possess.

Why They Are Detrimental:
Both emotions breed bitterness and conflict, obstructing spiritual tranquility. James 3:16 states, "For where you have envy and selfish ambition, there you find disorder and every evil practice."

Biblical Illustrations:

- Jealousy: Cain's jealousy of Abel led to his murder (Genesis 4:3-8).
- Envy: The Israelites were envious of the prosperity enjoyed by other nations, which led them to doubt God (Numbers 14:2-4).

Overcoming These Behaviors:

1. Celebrate the achievements of others.
2. Cultivate a mindset of gratitude and recognize God's provisions.
3. Refrain from comparing yourself to others.

Reflection Questions:

1. In what situations have I experienced feelings of jealousy or envy?

2. How do these feelings impact my relationships and my faith?

3. What steps can I take to replace envy with gratitude?

Practical Exercises:

1. Each day, write down three blessings in your life.

2. Offer genuine congratulations to someone this week.

3. Pray for contentment and joy in accordance with God's plan.

Closing Prayer:
Lord, free me from feelings of jealousy and envy, guiding me instead to rejoice in the blessings You bestow upon others.

Greedy

Chapter XVI
Greedy

Greed represents an excessive longing for wealth, possessions, or power that surpasses what is necessary or just. A greedy individual perpetually seeks more, irrespective of the needs of others or the repercussions of their choices. This tendency stems from selfishness, dissatisfaction, and a lack of trust in divine provision. Often, greed drives people to engage in dishonest behavior, hoard resources, or take advantage of others to fulfill their unquenchable desires.

The actions associated with greed are morally wrong as they elevate material wants over love, ethics, and concern for fellow beings. Greed fosters dishonesty, injustice, and even theft as individuals prioritize personal benefit over the welfare of others. It breeds discontentment since no quantity of wealth or possessions can genuinely satisfy a greedy heart. Furthermore, biblical teachings condemn greed as it signifies a deficiency in faith and appreciation for God's blessings.

Addressing the tendency toward greed is essential as it encourages generosity, harmony, and spiritual development. Overcoming greed enables individuals to share and appreciate what they possess rather than incessantly chasing after more. The elimination of greed nurtures healthy relationships and cultivates trust when integrity and fairness are evident to others. Additionally, correction allows individuals to concentrate on enduring values instead of fleeting worldly gains. If left unchecked, greed can lead to destruction, fractured relationships, and spiritual voids.

An illustration of greed in scripture can be found in 1 Timothy 6:9–10, which describes the love of money as the source of various evils. Those who chase after wealth recklessly may stray from their faith and inflict significant harm upon themselves. A notable example is Judas Iscariot's story in Matthew 26:14–16; he betrayed Jesus for thirty pieces of silver. Judas's avarice compelled him to commit a sinful act with irreversible consequences, showcasing the devastating impact of covetous desires.

To eradicate the habit of greed requires practicing contentment, generosity, and gratitude. Rather than endlessly seeking more possessions or wealth, individuals can focus on valuing what God has already provided them. By giving to others, supporting those in need, and sharing resources generously fosters a kind-hearted spirit. Engaging in prayer, exercising self-discipline, and reflecting on spiritual priorities aid in counteracting selfish tendencies. By choosing to find satisfaction in sufficiency while prioritizing God's will first, one can conquer greed and embrace a life characterized by peace, integrity, and love.

Greed

Definition: Greed refers to an overwhelming desire for wealth, possessions, or benefits at the cost of others.

Why It Is Wrong: Greed results in exploitation, wrongdoing, and a sense of dissatisfaction. Luke 12:15 warns, "Be cautious! Guard against all forms of greed; life is not defined by an abundance of material goods."

Why It Needs Correction: Greed promotes selfishness, dishonesty, and a lack of spiritual fulfillment.

Biblical Example: Judas Iscariot betrayed Jesus for thirty pieces of silver (Matthew 26:14-16).

Eliminating the Habit:
1. Cultivate generosity and a spirit of giving.
2. Reflect on the motivations behind financial choices.
3. Find contentment in what God provides.

Reflection Questions:
1. In what areas am I tempted to hoard for myself?
2. How can I allow generosity to counteract greed in my life?
3. What insights does Scripture offer regarding contentment?

Practical Exercises:
1. This week, offer assistance to someone in need.
2. Compile a list of non-material blessings that you cherish most.
3. Pray each day for a heart that embraces generosity.

Closing Prayer: Lord, liberate me from greed and guide me to be satisfied and generous with the resources You provide.

Wicked

Chapter XVII
Wicked

Wickedness refers to the conscious choice to engage in evil, hatred, or immoral behavior. A wicked individual takes pleasure in wrongdoing and frequently aims to harm others instead of offering assistance. This concept encompasses elements such as hatred, cruelty, deceit, and defiance against divine commands. Unlike errors stemming from human frailty, wickedness is a willful rejection of what is just. It corrupts the heart and incites harmful actions that affect both individuals and whole communities.

The nature of wickedness is fundamentally wrong as it contradicts principles of love, truth, and justice. Hatred, which often manifests as a consequence of wickedness, fractures relationships and fosters violence and animosity. Such wrongful acts erode trust and inflict suffering upon the innocent. Crucially, wickedness alienates individuals from God since He embodies holiness and cannot associate with evil. A life steeped in wickedness ultimately leads to condemnation and ruin rather than peace and blessings.

Addressing the tendency toward wickedness is essential; no society or individual can flourish when malevolence prevails. To foster peace among people, hatred must be substituted with love, while cruelty should give way to kindness. When wickedness is confronted effectively, families, communities, and nations are fortified through justice and empathy. Personal transformation also paves the way for healing and liberation from guilt. In contrast, failure to correct these tendencies allows wickedness to intensify and ensnare individuals in cycles of violence and sin.

A biblical illustration of wickedness is evident in the story of King Ahab and Queen Jezebel found in 1 Kings 21. Ahab coveted Naboth's vineyard; upon Naboth's refusal to sell it, Jezebel orchestrated a nefarious scheme involving false witnesses accusing Naboth of blasphemy—resulting in his death—and subsequently allowed Ahab to seize the vineyard. This narrative illustrates how wickedness driven by hate and selfish ambition culminated in murder and injustice. Ultimately, God held both Ahab and Jezebel accountable for their malevolent deeds.

To eradicate the habit of wickedness, individuals must turn towards God, repent for their wrongdoings, and actively cultivate love alongside righteousness. It is vital for people to choose forgiveness over hatred, compassion over cruelty, and truth over lies. Engaging in daily prayer, studying scripture, and surrounding oneself with positive influences can diminish the allure of wicked behavior. By seeking divine strength, individuals can conquer malevolent inclinations while living honorably before God. Ultimately, a life devoid of wickedness results in peace, joy, and eternal rewards.

Wickedness

Definition:
Wickedness refers to the tendency to engage in malevolent actions or harbor ill will, including feelings of hatred.

Why It Is Wrong:
Wickedness inflicts harm on others, undermines relationships, and incites divine judgment. As noted in Psalm 36:1-2, "Your wickedness instructs the wicked to behave sinfully; they are consumed with greed and cannot speak truthfully."

Why It Needs Correction:
If left unaddressed, wickedness can lead to spiritual deterioration and the breakdown of relationships.

Biblical Example:
King Herod exemplified wickedness by commanding the slaughter of innocent children (Matthew 2:16-18).

Eliminating the Habit:
1. Confess your sinful thoughts and behaviors to God.
2. Substitute hateful thoughts with love and forgiveness (Romans 12:21).
3. Surround yourself with influences that promote godliness.

Reflection Questions:
1. In what instances have I exhibited malice or wicked behavior?
2. How has hatred influenced my life or my relationships?
3. What actions can I take to foster love rather than wickedness?

Practical Exercises:
1. Pray for someone you find difficult to love.
2. Carry out one kind act each day as a substitute for negative behavior.
3. Reflect on scriptural passages that emphasize love and forgiveness.

Closing Prayer:
Lord, purify my heart from wickedness and fill me with Your love, mercy, and compassion.

Manipulator

Chapter XVIII
Manipulator

A manipulator is an individual who skillfully or unfairly influences or controls others, typically for their own benefit. This behavior encompasses deceit, coercion, or emotional exploitation to achieve desired outcomes. Although a manipulator may seem charismatic or convincing, their actions frequently harm others and foster distrust. Such conduct reveals traits of selfishness, dishonesty, and a lack of integrity.

Manipulation is fundamentally unethical because it takes advantage of and deceives others for personal gain. By treating individuals merely as tools to fulfill their objectives instead of recognizing them as unique persons, manipulators breach trust and damage relationships. This behavior leads to conflict, resentment, and confusion while potentially resulting in enduring negative effects for both the manipulator and those manipulated. The teachings of God encourage honesty, love, and fairness, thereby categorizing manipulation as sinful.

Addressing the tendency to manipulate is crucial for rebuilding trust, nurturing healthy relationships, and cultivating moral integrity. Those who cease manipulating others often adopt open communication practices, act with fairness, and respect the autonomy of people around them. This correction fosters peace and accountability by substituting self-serving strategies with sincerity and humility. If left unaddressed, manipulation can worsen into more severe forms of deceit such as lying, betrayal, or abuse.

An illustrative example from the Bible can be found in Genesis 27 when Jacob deceived his father Isaac to obtain the blessing intended for his brother Esau. With his mother's assistance, Jacob manipulated circumstances by disguising himself and lying to Isaac. This deception led to enduring family discord and highlights how manipulation can inflict harm and division. The narrative illustrates that God disapproves of employing deceit for personal gain.

The propensity for manipulation can be eradicated through the practice of honesty, transparency, and selflessness. Individuals should aim to communicate openly while respecting the rights and feelings of others and maintaining integrity in all situations. Engaging in prayer, self-reflection, and seeking accountability from trusted mentors can aid in overcoming manipulative behaviors. By transforming deceit into honesty and self-interest into service, one can conquer manipulation and cultivate relationships based on trust, respect, and love—thereby honoring God through their actions.

Manipulation

Definition
Manipulation refers to the act of influencing or controlling individuals for personal gain, often through deceitful or coercive means.

Why It Is Wrong
Manipulative actions breach trust, inflict harm, and disrespect divine principles. According to Proverbs 6:16-17, "There are six things the Lord detests... a person who schemes evil with deceit at heart."

Why It Needs Correction
Engaging in manipulation undermines relationships, damages credibility, and compromises spiritual integrity.

Biblical Example
Haman exerted manipulation over King Xerxes to issue a decree for the annihilation of the Jews (Esther 3:1-15).

Eliminating the Habit:
1. Foster honesty in your intentions and communication.
2. Surrender control and have faith in God's plans.
3. Pursue accountability within your relationships.

Reflection Questions:
1. In what situations have I resorted to manipulation to achieve my desires?
2. What impact does manipulation have on others and on my own conscience?
3. How can I choose to act with integrity instead?

Practical Exercises:
1. Analyze a recent event and identify any manipulative behaviors.
2. Aim for transparency in one interaction this week.
3. Pray for humility and sincerity in all your relationships.

Closing Prayer:
Lord, guide me to influence others through love and truth rather than through manipulation or deceit.

Promiscuous

Chapter XIX
Promiscuous

Being promiscuous refers to engaging in sexual encounters with various partners without the elements of commitment, responsibility, or adherence to divine principles regarding intimacy. This behavior often signifies a lack of self-discipline, neglect for moral standards, and a focus on personal pleasure. Such habits can lead to emotional, physical, and spiritual repercussions, negatively impacting relationships, trust levels, and individual character. Promiscuity tends to prioritize immediate gratification over lasting holiness and respect for oneself and others.

The act of promiscuity is considered wrong as it contradicts divine injunctions concerning sexual purity and fidelity. It may result in emotional turmoil, shattered trust, sexually transmitted diseases, and the disintegration of family units. Promiscuity diminishes the sanctity of relationships by reducing intimacy to mere self-indulgence. Biblical teachings consistently emphasize that sexual relations should be cherished within the confines of marriage; breaching this principle is viewed as sinful.

Addressing the tendency toward promiscuity is essential for safeguarding one's dignity, emotional health, and spiritual well-being.

Living without promiscuous behaviors enables individuals to form meaningful and committed relationships based on trust and mutual respect. Correcting such conduct also enhances self-control and aligns one's life with divine intentions. If left unaddressed, promiscuity can lead to further sinfulness, guilt accumulation, and fractured relationships that alienate individuals from God and others.

A biblical example illustrating promiscuity is found in the account of King David and Bathsheba in 2 Samuel 11:1–5. Despite being married, David's encounter with Bathsheba led him into adultery which spiraled into additional sins including orchestrating her husband Uriah's death. This narrative serves as a cautionary tale about how lust-driven promiscuous actions can have severe repercussions for both oneself and others while underscoring the importance of repentance.

Eliminating the habit of promiscuity involves cultivating self-control, honoring oneself and others, along with adhering to divine principles. Steering clear of tempting situations, seeking guidance from trustworthy mentors, and concentrating on spiritual development can aid in replacing promiscuous behaviors with purity. Engaging in prayer, studying sacred texts, and establishing healthy boundaries within relationships are vital strategies for overcoming this inclination. By honoring divine teachings through disciplined living, individuals can achieve lives characterized by sexual integrity, self-respect, and inner peace.

Promiscuity

Definition: Promiscuity refers to engaging in sexual activities that deviate from God's intended design, characterized by a lack of commitment and respect.

Why It Is Wrong: Such behavior can result in emotional distress, spiritual degradation, and damage to interpersonal relationships. According to 1 Corinthians 6:18-20, "Flee from sexual immorality. All other sins a person commits are outside the body, but whoever sins sexually, sins against their own body. Do you not know your bodies are temples of the Holy Spirit?"

Why It Needs Correction: Engaging in promiscuous behavior often leads to fractured relationships, feelings of guilt, and increased spiritual vulnerability.

Biblical Example: The harlot Rahab provided protection for God's people but later repented and aligned herself with God's intentions (Joshua 2:1-21).

Eliminating the Habit:
1. Seek purity and establish accountability.
2. Set clear boundaries to avoid temptations.
3. Replace lustful actions with activities centered on God.

Reflection Questions:
1. In what areas do I feel tempted to stray from God's sexual design?
2. How can I safeguard my heart and body for His purpose?
3. Who can assist me in my pursuit of purity?

Practical Exercises:
1. Recognize triggers and eliminate sources of temptation.
2. Pray for the strength to honor God with your physical being.
3. Look for accountability from a trusted mentor or spiritual advisor.

Closing Prayer:
Lord, guide me in honoring You through my body and relationships as I strive for purity and self-discipline.

Angry

Chapter XX
Angry

Anger is a powerful emotional reaction to perceived offenses, injustices, or feelings of frustration. While experiencing anger is not inherently sinful, the tendency toward uncontrolled or chronic anger can become harmful when it results in destructive actions, unkind words, or lingering resentment. Individuals who frequently succumb to anger often find their emotions dictating their behavior, which can lead to damaged relationships, impaired judgment, and spiritual turmoil.

The manifestation of uncontrolled anger is problematic, as it has the potential to inflict harm on both oneself and others. Such persistent anger frequently fosters conflict, bitterness, and even violence. It can erode trust, dismantle relationships, and establish an environment filled with fear and tension. The Bible cautions against allowing anger to dictate one's actions; for instance, Ephesians 4:26–27 states: "Be angry and do not sin; do not let the sun go down on your anger; do not give the devil a foothold." This indicates that while anger may be a natural response, it must be handled in accordance with divine principles.

Addressing the issue of uncontrolled anger is

crucial for sustaining peace, emotional well-being, and a character aligned with godly values. By learning to respond in a calm and deliberate manner, individuals can resolve disputes instead of exacerbating them. This correction promotes effective communication, builds trust, and nurtures healthy relationships. Failing to confront this habit may result in enduring bitterness, regret, and estrangement from God and others.

A biblical illustration of anger occurs in Exodus 32:19 when Moses became enraged upon witnessing the Israelites worshiping the golden calf. In his fury, he shattered the stone tablets that held the Ten Commandments. Although Moses' anger stemmed from righteous indignation, it also exemplifies how powerful emotions can prompt hasty decisions. This narrative underscores the necessity of managing one's anger with wisdom and self-discipline to prevent harmful consequences.

The tendency towards habitual anger can be transformed or moderated through the practice of patience, self-control, and forgiveness. Engaging in prayer, meditating on scripture, and reflecting on personal triggers can aid individuals in responding thoughtfully rather than reacting impulsively. Embracing forgiveness, releasing resentment, and pursuing constructive conflict resolution are essential steps toward overcoming detrimental anger. By fostering an attitude of peace and patience within themselves, individuals can replace unchecked anger with love, understanding, and divine wisdom.

Anger

Definition: Anger refers to the tendency to let feelings of wrath, resentment, or uncontrolled frustration dictate one's reactions.

Why It Is Wrong: Allowing anger to take hold can lead to sin, damaged relationships, and spiritual distress. As stated in Ephesians 4:26-27, "In your anger do not sin: Do not let the sun go down while you are still angry, and do not give the devil a foothold."

Why It Needs Correction: Unchecked anger undermines trust, disrupts peace, and harms fellowship.

Biblical Example: Moses exhibited anger upon witnessing the Israelites worship the golden calf, which led to significant repercussions (Exodus 32:19-20).

Eliminating the Habit:
1. Cultivate patience and self-control through prayer.
2. Approach conflicts with calmness and aim for swift resolutions.
3. Substitute feelings of frustration with gratitude and a broader perspective.

Reflection Questions:
1. What situations trigger my anger most frequently?

2. In what ways has uncontrolled anger impacted my relationships or spiritual wellbeing?
3. What actionable steps can I adopt to respond calmly rather than react in anger?

Practical Exercises:
1. When feeling angry, take a moment to pause and pray for tranquility before reacting.
2. Keep a journal documenting instances that provoke anger and contemplate Godly responses.
3. Commit to memory and meditate on verses related to patience and self-control (e.g., Proverbs 15:1).

Closing Prayer:
Lord, grant me the ability to manage my anger, respond with patience, and embody Your peace in every circumstance.

Conclusion

Conclusion

Toxic habits represent harmful behaviors or patterns that adversely impact an individual's life, relationships, and spiritual health. These actions encompass lying, jealousy, greed, manipulation, anger, and other detrimental behaviors that inflict harm on both oneself and others. Typically arising from selfishness, pride, dissatisfaction, or a lack of self-discipline, toxic habits can obstruct personal development and spiritual growth. Recognizing these toxic behaviors is the initial step toward overcoming them.

Such habits are considered negative as they contravene divine principles, cause harm to others, and undermine relationships. Actions like gossiping and jealousy not only erode trust but also incite conflict and division. They can lead to emotional, spiritual, and at times physical damage. Engaging in these habits distances individuals from God and disrupts the peaceful and loving connections He intends for them. The repercussions of toxic habits illustrate the necessity of acknowledging and addressing them to lead a virtuous life.

Addressing toxic habits is essential for maintaining personal integrity, fostering spiritual development, and nurturing healthy relationships. As individuals strive to amend destructive behaviors, they cultivate qualities such as honesty, patience, humility, and love. This process of correction enables one to substitute harmful tendencies with constructive habits that encourage trust, peace, and joy. Failing to rectify toxic habits may result in repetitive mistakes and persistent conflict in one's own life as well as in the lives of others.

The elimination of toxic habits can be achieved through self-awareness, discipline, and reliance on divine guidance. Effective strategies include prayer, engaging with Scripture, self-reflection, seeking accountability from others, and consciously practicing positive behaviors. By identifying triggers for these habits and making deliberate choices while asking for assistance when necessary, individuals can liberate themselves from destructive cycles. Replacing toxic practices with healthier actions enhances character development as well as strengthens relationships and faith.

In summary, it is crucial to recognize that toxic habits are damaging behaviors requiring attention and rectification. They negatively affect relationships, dishonor God's intentions for humanity, and hinder personal growth. By identifying these harmful patterns and replacing them with positive actions aligned with divine principles, individuals can attain peace of mind along with integrity and spiritual maturity. Overcoming such challenges necessitates deliberate effort combined with humility and dependence on God; however, the outcome is a transformed existence characterized by lovefulness fidelity—and enduring positive change.

About The Author

About The Author

Brenda Diann Johnson was born in Dallas, Texas on September 14, 1970 to Robert Johnson and Thelma Byrd. She is the oldest of five children. She has a brother, sister, and two half brothers.

Brenda received her education from the Dallas and Wharton, Texas school systems. She graduated from Government, Law, and Law Enforcement Magnet High School in Dallas. She also received her Bachelor of Arts degree in Communications (Broadcast News) from UTA in Arlington, Texas and her Masters of Education Degree from Strayer University. She has her Texas license in Life, Health, Accident & HMO insurance, her Texas Adjusters License in All Lines, and she is a Texas Notary Public.

Today, Brenda is the CEO/Founder of The Young Scholar's Book Club and ASWIFTT ENTERPRISES, LLC. She is also an experienced educator who has taught and tutored Pre-K through College. Brenda is the Dean of Education, Curriculum & Instruction for Best Practices Training Institute (B.P.T.I). She has also authored books and articles.

From 2001 to 2002, Brenda served as the chairperson for an entrepreneur group called STEP (Sowing Toward Everlasting Prosperity) and as a Center Leader for the Plan Fund.

She also served as the Co-Founder of ASWIFTT Writer's Guild from 2010 to 2019.

In the community, she has served as a volunteer to organizations that help AIDS, HIV, and Syphilis patients.

Brenda currently lives in Texas with her family.

Books and Services
ASWIFTT ENTERPRISES, LLC

Business advertising for Print & Media
BOOK PUBLISHING
RADIO
T.V.
Newspaper

We have affordable advertising packages in our media categories. Some Ads are as low as $35.00. Email to ask about our Business Ads and Commercials.

You can visit us online or e-mail us:
www.aswifttbooks.com
aswifttbookpublishing@yahoo.com

ASWIFTT BOOKS

(Ambassadors Sent With Information For This Time)

ASWIFTT ENTERPRISES, LLC creates businesses that write and publish in all three (3) media genres such as radio, tv, and newspaper that focus on delivering timely, newsworthy and accurate news stories. The media genres also report on local, regional, national and international topics.

The Young Scholar's Workbook: Book I Vol. I (www.tysbookclub.com)

The Young Scholar's Workbook: Book I Vol. I

By Brenda Diann Johnson

This is a fundraiser publication for The Young Scholar's Book Club. 50% of the proceeds go to help keep mentoring and tutoring services free to students. $19.95 plus s/h

How Did I Get Into This Mess? You Compromised, Saith the Lord 2nd Edition

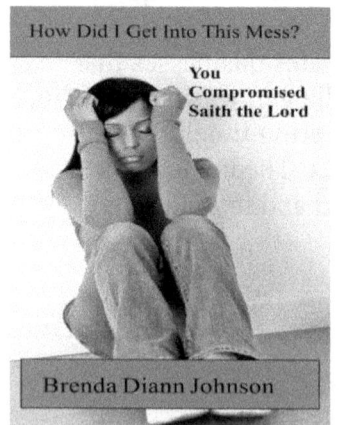

How Did I Get Into This Mess? You Compromised, Saith the Lord 2nd Edition by

Brenda Diann Johnson

$12.95 plus s/h

Articles for Personal Growth and Development: Volume I

Articles for Personal Growth and Development: Vol. I by

Brenda Diann Johnson

$9.95 plus s/h

My Baby Sister

My Baby Sister by

Brenda Diann Johnson

$15.95 plus s/h

Available in English and Spanish

Advertise in
ASWIFTT BOOKS

Your business will have a permanent advertising spot in an ASWIFTT Book. The book that carries your Business Ad will continue to advertise your business every time the book is printed and purchased by a customer. For more information on ASWIFTT ENTERPRISES book advertising email us at: aswifttbookpublishing@yahoo.com

$35.00 Business Ad
Includes:
Business Name
Address

$100.00 Business Ad
Includes:
Logo
Business Name
Address
Phone Number
Website
Short Bio

$65.00 Business Ad
Includes:
Logo
Business Name
Address
Phone Number
Website

ASWIFTT ENTERPRISES, LLC ORDER FORM

Name_____

Address_____

City_____

State_____

Zip_____
Item _____Amount_____
Item _____Amount_____
Item _____Amount_____

Add $8.50 for Shipping and Handling on books
Total:_____

Make Checks, Money Orders, Cashier's Checks out to:

ASWIFTT ENTERPRISES, LLC

P.O. Box 380669

Duncanville, Texas 75138

Credit Card Orders:
Circle One: Master Card   Visa   American Express Discover
Credit Card Number_____
Exp. Date_____
Three Digit Security Number on back of
Card_____

Name & Address Associated with Credit Card:

Authorization Signature_____Date_____

Your order will be processed or shipped 2 to 4 weeks from the date order is received. Direct concerns on orders email: aswifttbookpublishing@yahoo.com
You can also order online at: www.aswifttbooks.com

Thank you for your business! Make copies of this form.

www.ingramcontent.com/pod-product-compliance
Lightning Source LLC
Chambersburg PA
CBHW060828050426
42453CB00008B/623